WORDS GO OUT TO PLAY

wo**r**ds

go
out
to
play

ADRIAN LANCINI

EDWARD FENTON

JOHN LANYON

ROB STEPNEY

THE CHARLBURY PRESS

First published in 2018 by
The Charlbury Press, Orchard Piece,
Crawborough, Charlbury,
Oxfordshire, OX7 3TX
www.day-books.com

ISBN 978-0-9546342-6-1

Design and illustration by Adrian Lancini

Printed in Great Britain by
CPI Antony Rowe (UK) Ltd.,
Croydon CR0 4YY

GREETINGS FROM THE AUTHORS

Collect their signatures here

IT'S A BOOK!

....

Adrian Lancini

CONGRATULATIONS ON YOUR NEW EDITION!

....

Edward Fenton

GET WELL VERSED SOON!

....

John Lanyon

MANY HAPPY PAGE TURNS!

....

Rob Stepney

A writer's notebook: the horror of the opening page

The feint lines taunt me
Potential greatness lies between them
But so does the grim prospect of mediocrity
The cosmos reduced to mind, hand, pen, paper
The ghosts of Shelley and Byron watch on
As the nib plunders virgin paper
And ink is spilled

On emergence

from the cloud
all raindrops will be assessed for symmetry
non-standard drops will be returned
for a fresh start
raindrops which linger
taking in the view
will be accelerated
less than transparent raindrops
will be polished before release
lonely raindrops will be integrated
freezing raindrops will be warmed
to a minimum of five degrees Centigrade
raindrops with excessive, show-off surface tension
will be counselled
raindrops will not slide down window panes
raindrops will be proud of their patch of sky
failing clouds will be renamed
raindrops congregating in rainbows
will be dispersed
raindrops from nimbostratus clouds
will be viewed with suspicion.

No more puddles
no more splashing
no more reflections

THE rovidence
OF BIRDS

Said the pigeon from the wood

'Take two cows, Taffy,

'Take two cows, Taffy. Take.'

'Which two, and where to?'

Asked the owl

'To the Ark, Ark, Ark'

Answered the raven.

And so the cows were taken to the Ark

And they were saved

From the Flood.

Adjectives
tenses
clauses
empathy
diction
rhymes
similes
irony
metrical feet
metaphors
assonance
vocabulary

trimmed
tightened
conditioned
toned
polished
cleansed
plucked
coloured
moisturised
extended
waxed
volumised

How beautiful
your poetry
is today.

11

Salon

The Soul's Last Words to the Heart

I know you don't believe
in the soul, but sometimes
I struggle to believe in the body

It was when you were gone
that I noticed you most
Disappearing round the corner,
or somewhere in a crowd

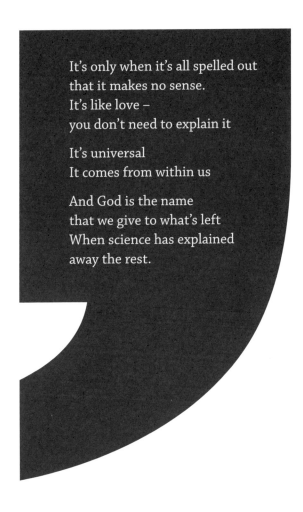

It's only when it's all spelled out
that it makes no sense.
It's like love –
you don't need to explain it

It's universal
It comes from within us

And God is the name
that we give to what's left
When science has explained
away the rest.

The campsite sign read

NO FIRES

So I built one in my mind
I used my earliest memories
for scrunched-up bits of newspaper
My schoolboy memories for kindling
And my adult memories for firewood
But I couldn't think of anything to use as a match
So I just stared at my unlit fire
Until dawn brought a new day.

The campsite sign read

NO CAMPING

I was confused so I took out my iPhone
    and visited www.confused.com
But that just banged on about insurance
Which confused me further
So I got in my car and drove to another campsite
Their sign read:

CAMPING ALLOWED, BUT ONLY WITH INSURANCE

So I took out my iPhone and revisited www.confused.com
But they didn't offer insurance for camping trips
So I got back in my car and drove to a place
    that didn't have any signs or any Wi-Fi*
And everything made perfect sense.

*page 130

FOR OUR TIMES

A MESSAGE

*From the
great Basilica
of Sacré-Cœur*

The sign said:
Please enter
only if you
wish to
pray.

Somewhat to my surprise,
it seemed an OK offer and I
went in and sat. Even the forbidden
flash photography seemed dimmed
and call tones moderately muted.
Under the great dome of Christ in Splendour,
the sky as richly blue as the robe of the Virgin.
A Pope, improbably, offers to renounce the
wealth of the world; a nun gives up her crown.
Three bishops in a selfie hold up Sacré-Cœur itself
as offering. An angel surrenders his licence to fly.

And then my
mobile went off.
It was not God
answering my call.
It was Vodafone
with a message
for our times. I had
been insufficiently
attentive to the
earthly rewards
I'd earned and
must do better.

I left,
humbled by
stupidity. Down
the many steps, back on
the streets. As penance, I chose
the emptiest of Moroccan restaurants.
But I never understood why Leila had
so little custom since she had cooked a
near-miraculous Lamb of God tagine.

to
be

'w' stem (was, were)
'a' stem (am, are)
'b' stem (be, being, been)
'i' stem (is)

The strongest, most irregular of verbs,
washed in a long tide,
brought to a slow boil,
waving two fingers at predictability.

This is how she does existence.

f

l   e

Cars graze
sacred fields

electric lights
rise
ON
steel towers

HIGH fences
guarantee
you and I
never meet

pay to be
| a prisoner |

injured
twisted
bro   ken
music
slips through
the mesh.

a   s

v   t

i

**So you think
you can use me**
Reuse, and reduce
Then bin me one Tuesday
When you've got no more use.

**You can try
to discard me**
But I won't disappear
The laws of thermodynamics
Mean I'll always be here.

**I'll be there
in your compost**
All plastic and card
I may look biodegradable
But inside I'm too hard.

**And you think
that I'll break down**

But that's where you're wrong
I may look biodegradable
But inside I'm still strong.

I was chewing the fat with my newspaper editor, Gordon Bennett, when he asked 'Could you write me an article about peculiar phrases and expressions?'

'Piece of cake,' I replied. I was three sheets to the wind at the time – been on the mother's ruin you see.

I won't beat around the bush, my first attempt at the article was a load of cobblers. I made a dog's dinner of the next one too. My third attempt had me pleased as Punch before I lost the plot and it all went pear-shaped.

I should have taken it all with a pinch of salt but instead it was really getting my goat. I thought it would have been easy as pie, but no, it was proving to be a dickens of a job.

I was desperate to cut the mustard, but I just kept making a pig's ear of it. Damp squib after damp squib. I don't mind spilling the beans here – I almost gave up the ghost.

In the end it took donkeys' years but I finally hit the nail on the head.

I went back to square one, separated the wheat from the chaff and Bob's your uncle ... I had my article.

And if you'll pardon my French, it was the dog's bollocks.

A PIECE OF CAKE

The
swell of
summer

ther-
mal

the
spine of
summer

the
edge
of it

the
lighted
shoulders
of the
standing
stones

AT THE ROLLRIGHT STONES

The King's Men

                                        just
                                          touching
                            warmth
                            and
                            weight

                        faces
                        and
                        gestures
                        close
                        together

                    the
                    story
                    and the
          the   curse
          falling
  lines   sun
  of barley
  stubble

'Traditionally a monarch and his courtiers petrified by a witch,
the Rollright Stones consist of three groups: the King's Men stone
circle; the Whispering Knights burial chamber; and the single
King Stone.' – English Heritage.
  The Rollright Stones are located on the Oxfordshire/Warwickshire
border SP 2963 3089.

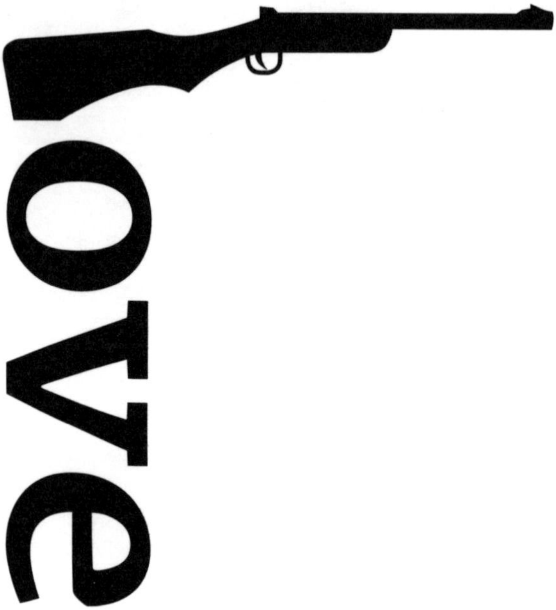
ove

hearts

The clouds, in the darkening dusk
Are stacked one
                above
                another
Like sugary Love Hearts
Sherbet yellow, pink and then
The purple of an elderberry stain

The bare branches
Of the solitary beech
Cradle the rising moon
To its lonely heart
An image so perfect
I too want to hold it

The happy hunter, meanwhile,
Walks home from the wood
Sheathed gun over his shoulder
Dead pigeons slung on his belt.

On grey feathers
Bright spots of blood
Their hearts splattered.

Leaves moistened by the same mist
Watered by the same rain
Their petals open to the same sun
The same snow covers them in winter
And they wake to the same spring birds
Their roots mingle and enrich
Three flowers grow together in Bosnian soil.

For Lorenc
Tjentište 2014

flowers

of Sutjeska

MAY
29

Q: IS A PATH THE WISDOM OF MANY FEET?

It seemed obvious to me that a path is the wisdom of many feet. But I asked smart-phone, smart-arse Siri if others thought that this was true. He paused.   Then he replied by saying that a birth was the wisdom of many feet. When he'd finally understood the question, this is what he told me:

Buy *Inspirations from Ancient Wisdom* –

At the feet of the master, there is light on the path (*Krishnamurti@amazon. co.uk*). Do not set foot on the path of the wicked (*From Proverbs 4 verse 14*).

I will teach you wisdom's ways and lead you in straight paths. When you walk your steps will not be hampered. (*From Proverbs 4 verse 11*). The Wisdom Path was formerly known as the Heart Sutra (*The Hong Kong Tourist Board*); and – A path is a public walkway; many people clear it over a period of time (*I think that was a town planner*). So I asked Google. Is a path the widsom of many feet? It asked me 'Do you mean "Is a path the wisdom of many feet"?' Of course I did! And Google came back with the same Proverbs and the same Town Planner.

Is this a stitch-up? I thought. Surely a path *is* the wisdom of many feet. But technology didn't seem so sure – could I be on the wrong track?

FINDING MYSELF ALONE

IN THE MUSEUM

The tarnished coins
the fragments of pottery
the corroded weapons
the long-lost jewellery
don't worry –
someone will discover you
someone will try to understand
someone will hold you
someone will treasure you …
… it's just a question of time.

We are all

On a bombed-out piece of wasteland
That had once been a park
Twenty boys are being drilled in the rain.
Twenty schoolboys, all in the brown and black
of the Deutsches Jungvolk –
All but you. Your parents wouldn't buy you the uniform.

And as the boys are put through their paces,
A stranger appears. He stops and watches
From behind the fence. Ashen-faced
He's fixed on you. Then furtively he beckons you over.
You're in two minds, but it's best to obey grown-ups …
People have been shot for less.

He doesn't speak, but he hands you something cold ⟶

continuing

Rhabarberkuchen.
It's years since you last saw rhubarb –
Not since the war started. You don't even like it,
And it's soggy, sodden from the rain.

He's probably been carrying it around for days, saving it,
And now seeing you without a uniform
He can turn it into a symbol of resistance
A piece of hope he can share.

It's his way of saying: 'You and me both.
I hate the Nazis –
        those bastards who've fucked up our lives.
You know they killed my brother? He was a doctor.
Refused to conduct some experiments.
They took my son too. Sent his regiment to Russia ...

God knows what happened there. He never came back.
So don't give in, boy. Be yourself – and good luck.'

the journeys

That's what he wants to say, but daren't,
Or he could be murdered too.
So he shows you in the only way he can, and moves on.

What happened to that man, and to the other boys –
Did they survive the war? Who knows.
But you survived,
And as soon as you were old enough
You left Germany to escape the threat of wars to come.
You sailed to Australia
First Melbourne, then Adelaide, where they needed workers.

For a year you lived in a tent
Saving your wages to buy a bicycle.
You were a good worker.
You met an English girl,
You married, and had a daughter.
A new life.

# of others ......

But the war never left you.
You struggled constantly to make sense of it,
Of what it had done to you and your generation.
You wished you'd had a proper education,
Not starting each lesson with a chant of 'Heil Hitler'.
You could have been a boxer – you showed promise –
But that was all messed up too.
So many regrets.

And sorry, but you were a hard man to get on with.
Opinionated, controlling, always so critical of others,
Resentful of those who'd had it easier than you.
Even when you told me about that day in the rain
It was like 'What did I want with that geezer's cake?' –
Just one more thing that made no sense
Not the act of defiance
That will stay with me for ever.

GHOST · Writing

the GHOST writer

(with John Lanyon)

I imagine me
computer-bound,
cigarette ash between the keys
coffee machine on repeat play
I meet me a couple of times
I'm nothing like I look on TV
big spaces
short chapters
in time for Christmas
a bookshop mountain of me
before tastes change
the difficult childhood
that thing that happened
the big break
that thing that went wrong
meeting so-and-so
a few grammatical mistakes
for authenticity
I am other people
I could write a book.

On 13 April 2017, the Sheffield Star reported
an 'unnamed' motorist claimed to have seen
a toucan fly past him on a Sheffield street.
This sparked a huge toucan hunt in the city.
After many days of searching the exotic bird was
finally tracked down by reporters as it hopped
away from the city's Crucible Theatre.

When questioned what it was doing in Sheffield,
this is what the toucan said:

IN GREGGS WE TRUST

A toucan in
SHEFFIELD

TWINNED WITH A CHAFFINCH IN SÃO PAULO

I'd heard talk of a forest in Nottingham
That was my original destination
But I overshot the M1 turn-off
Found myself in Trowell, at the Moto Service Station

After two cans of Lilt – they had an offer on –
I took flight and had barely left the ground
When I thought I saw a sign for the Beak District
So on I went, northbound

Forty miles later, something caught my eye
A lavish domed temple, hundreds of feet tall
A place where humans worshipped
Its name was Meadowhall

Inside I couldn't believe my luck
A River Island, a Timberland and a Monsoon!
I felt so at home here
I stayed all afternoon

In Waterstones I met a puffin and a penguin
They took me under their wings
We went into Wetherspoon's
And drank all manner of things

The booze made me peckish
I hadn't eaten since my morning eggs
The penguin perked up and said
'Hey guys, let's go to

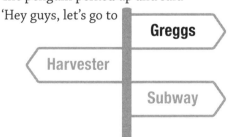

Everything there looked so tasty
I just didn't know what to get
Then the puffin recommended

The tuna sweetcorn baguette

It was amazing – the tuna was symphonious
And the sweetcorn was so ... sweet
The penguin said I should head for Sheffield
There's a Greggs on every street

'But where would I stay?' I asked
The penguin pondered and replied
'Well, there's a theatre called the Crucible
Where once a Parrott thrived'

To the Crucible I flew
But on arrival I overheard
The theatre was showing Cats
Well, that's no place for a bird

So I'm heading

SOUTH

for Nottingham
What I originally set out to do
For not only is there a forest
Gregg has shops there too

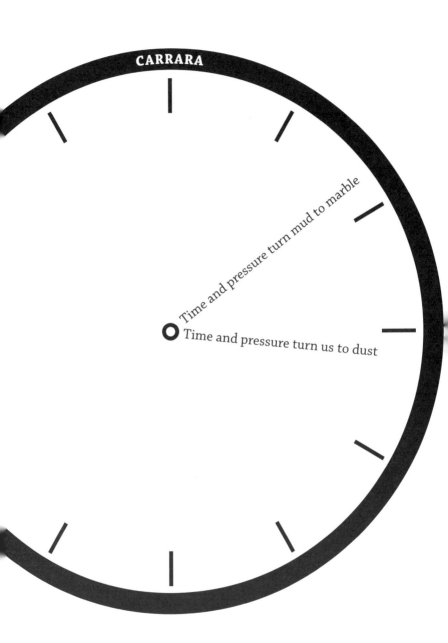

CARRARA

Time and pressure turn mud to marble

Time and pressure turn us to dust

1. When were lions red?
2. What's inside a Saracen's head?

3. Why do horseshoes come in threes?
4. Is it lucky to cross your keys?

5. Can you really trust a dog and gun?
6. What's the perfect setting for a rising sun?

7. What justifies calling an old inn new?
8. What made the boar turn from brown to blue?

9. Will the bird in hand ever fly free?
10. What makes an oak royalty?

11. What on earth is a barley mow?
12. Where do the coach and horses go?

13. Does the green man smoke dope?
14. Why should an anchor bring us hope?

15. Doesn't an eagle and child ring alarms?
16. What is the meat in the butcher's arms?

17. Is Mount Pleasant a nice place to stay?
18. Why is the house only halfway?

19. Which groom married a horse?
20. Does the shoulder of mutton come with sauce?

Tie-break question! First to shout –
Is the cock inn or is the cock out?

pub quiz

1. ....
2. ....
3. ....
4. ....
5. ....
6. ....
7. ....
8. ....
9. ....
10. ....
11. ....
12. ....
13. ....
14. ....
15. ....
16. ....
17. ....
18. ....
19. ....
20. ....

<small>ON</small> <small>THE</small> Horizon

I am building a lighthouse
at the edge of things;
land, sea and sky's meeting
night and day
woman and man.

The walls rise in an elegant curve,
a tree where trees don't grow.

I build to show structures
may be built in difficult places,
to signal a presence,
a unique pattern in light and darkness.

AN
UNSEEN
HAND

There
IS AN
unseen
HAND
that crafts
A CAIRN
Simple in design,
MODEST IN PROPORTION
But it points to
THE STARS

ALFA
ROMEO

KNOWS WHERE THE CAR GOES

Enchanted golden cottages with secret courtyard gardens
Wooden beams and inglenooks and latches, not locks
With names like Phoenix
Anvil and Lavender
Wychwood and Wormwood, Middlewell and Fox

Stately Georgian houses with sage-green paintwork
Panelled halls and drawing-rooms and smooth cut stone
With names like Grantchester
Oxford and Marlborough
Prospect and Redding Wyck and the Queen's Own

But there's one thing they're all short of –
    parking space and garages –
Not like the postwar semi or the modern bungalow
With names like Tregonwell
Gracecroft and Ralphland
Livanya, Kipkelion and Con Brio.

You left me a broken loom
two-thirds of a beautiful, ancient thing
missing the beam, the heddles, the castle –
a harp that has lost its strings –
missing the click-clack,
the criss-cross, the up-down,
missing an eye for colour
a rhythm in repetition
a careful, organising hand.

I think of you at the loom
your thick black hair
fixed with knitting needles
into an unfashionable bun.

sing

You taught me to make from instinct
that the surprise of beauty comes
when one thing crosses another, again and again.

There are magical houses of making
where creation turns like a prayer wheel
a spinning wheel, a mill wheel;
where we make with broken things
with lost parts
with broken hearts;
where music rises unbeckoned
from harps that have lost their strings.

ON THE PASSING OF THE F1350APW

(THE STATESMAN ALPINE FRIDGE FREEZER)

It came containerised on a slow boat from China to Gloucester Docks. Rebadged as a 'Statesman' (how diplomatic), it hides its origins well.

The pictograms

on its broken thermostat

give the game away.

A+

Calling itself 'Alpine'

it dreams of snuggling up to cows

rolling in the snow

picking an Edelweiss.

IT · GORGES · ON
ELECTRICITY · FREEZING
THE · CELERY · TO
A · MUSH

The repairman did his best but you can't get the parts.

In Asia, white is the colour of mourning.

The world warms. Life gets colder.

I think of the ancestors arriving in sailing ships. Gold-lacquered boxes with scenes of flowers, leaves, birds, gardens –

red-painted cabinets with stout brass fittings whose very beauty promised survival.

2018/F1350APW

Dear old Oxford –
A poem
from the future

Oxford, England 2118

A man called David Coleman (no relation to the former TV presenter of the defunct pastime known as 'sport') wins the reality game show 'Limitless Cousins'. His prize is anything he desires.

David's wish is to re-write the English language with a completely new alphabet. Being a poet, the first thing David does in new English is to write a poem comparing his home city of Oxford to how it was back in 2018.

The following is said poem, first appearing in this new form of English and then translated back into the old language.

NB Many place names and some words that have become obsolete remain the same, as do a few words that David simply forgot to translate.

ⵚⳑⁿ⅃⳦ ꞉ ⵔ⌠⥩ⵡ Oxford

ⵔⳑ⟨⳦꞉⳦ ⵔⳑⵏⳑ ⴷⱴ⫽⫽ⵔⵡ ⫽⟨ⳑ Pitt-Rivers ⴲⵓⵎⵍⳑ⭢ⵎ,
⟨Ⳑ꞉⳦⳦ ⵖⴲ⭤⪫ⵍⵖⵓⵔⳑ ⳑ⳨⟨⳦⫽꞉⳨ ⵖⵖⵏ
ⳑⵔⵔ ⵍⵏ⫽ⵍ ⫽⟨⳦ National ⴲⵓⵍⳑ⭢ⵎ ⵔⳑ ⟨Ⳑ꞉⳦ⵍⳑ Air
⟨ⵏ⟨꞉ ⵔⳑ⟨ⵏⳑ ⵔⳑ ⳑⵏⵓⳑ ⫽ⵔ ⫽.ⵖ⳨

ⵔⳑ⟨⳦꞉⳦ ⵔⳑⵏⳑ ⫽⟨⳦ Bodleian Library
ⳑⵔⵍⵍⴲⳑⴲ ⫽⟨ⳑⵍⵍⵖⵓⴲⵍ ⵔⳑ ⵍⳑ⟨ⵏⵍⳑ books
⟨⫽ ⳑⵔⵔ ⵍⵏ⫽ⵣⵍ⳦ⵍ ⵔ⟨ⵔⵍⳑⴲ replicas ⵔⳑ ⵔⵍ꞉ⵍⳑⳑⵓⳑ⳨⳦ⵍ
⟨ⵏ⟨꞉ ⵔⳑⳑⳑ ⵔⳑⳑⵏⳑ ⟨ⵔⵍ⫽⫽ ⵔⵍ꞉ ⟨ⵔⵔⳑⵍ

ⵔⳑ⟨⳦꞉⳦ ⵔⳑⵏⳑ, underneath ⫽⟨⳦ ⥩⳨ⴲⳑⳑⳑ ⵔⳑ ⵍⳑⳑⵍ
students ⵔⵍⵍⵏⴲ ⟨Ⳑ꞉⳦ⳑⵔⵏ⳨ ⳑ꞉ⵔⵖⵎ
ⳑⵔⵔ ⫽.ⵖⵍⳑ꞉ⵔⵔ Apple ⟨Ⳑ꞉ⵔⵔⵔⵔⵍⵍⵍ
ⵖ⳨ⵔⵖⵍⵔⵖⵏⵔⳑ ⟨ⳑ ⥩ⵔⵖ⳦ⵝ, ⵔⳑⵍ⫽⟨ⳑ ⵖⳑⴲ chrome

ⵔⳑ⟨⳦꞉⳦ ⵔⳑⵏⳑ ⵔⳑ ⫽⫽ⵔⵝ ⵍⴲⵏⵍⵍⵔⳑ ⫽ⵍⵔⳑⵖⵍ꞉ⵍⳐ꞉⳦ⵍ,
ⵍⵍⵍ꞉ⵔⵔⵔⵍⳑⳑ ⟨ⴲ⟨⳦꞉ ⫽⟨ⳑ꞉ⵔ꞉ⵍⳑⳑ Christ ⵔⳑ꞉ⵍ꞉ⵔⳑ Meadows
ⳑⵔⵔ ⵔⳑ ⫽⫽ⵖⳑⵝ ⵖ hallucinogen ⵔⵖ⟨ⵔⵔⳑⴲ ⵝⳑⳑ⳦⭤⪫⫽ ꞉⳨
ⵖ ⳑⳑⳑⳑ⫽⫽ⵔⵖ⟨ⵔⵔ⳨ ⵎⵔⴲⳑ ⳑⴲ frog ⵍⳑⵔ⳦꞉⫽⟨ⳑⴲ ⵏ⫽⫽. ⫽⟨⳦ ⳑⵔⵍⳑⳑ

Oxford … London
£15 … £7.50 …
… intergalactic …
… Milton Keynes

… Cowley …
… Pad Thai … Jalfrezi
… hologram … Guy
… Maisie

… Sheldonian Theatre
… musicians …
…
…

… Headington
… sticking …

… Headington
… sticking …
… failed …
… fish
… Oxford …

Dear Old Oxford

Where once stood the Pitt-Rivers Museum,
free admission every day
Now sits the National Museum of Fresh Air
for which we have to pay

Where once the Bodleian Library
housed thousands of unique books
It now stores cloned replicas of ourselves
for when we've lost our looks

Where once, underneath the Bridge of Sighs
students would freely roam
Now patrol Apple iRobocops
available in black, white and chrome

Where once we took simple pleasures,
strolling idly through Christ Church Meadows
Now we take a hallucinogen called Kermit 9
a genetically modified frog, snorted up the nose

Where once we caught the Oxford Tube to London
£15 for adults, £7.50 for under-fifteens
Now we pay 70,000 dollars for intergalactic rides
via Bicester Village, Bicester and Milton Keynes

Where once the Cowley Road
greeted us with aromas of a Pad Thai or a Jalfrezi
Now we're met by a hologram pimp called Guy
and virtual prostitutes called Maisie

Where once graced the Sheldonian Theatre
for renowned classical musicians to play
Now looms the statue of Riyad Neshnicov
the 68th President of the USA

Where once stood a house in Headington
with a shark sticking out of its roof ...

There still stands a house in Headington
with a shark sticking out if its roof
Yes, so much of this once great City has failed to survive
But at least a headless carbon-fibre fish
is keeping 'Dear Old Oxford' alive.

W*I*TH*DRAWAL*

In a thirty-Euro hotel in Montmartre
In a bedside drawer
A blister pack of buprenorphine
I hope you said goodbye
From here on in

AT THE ROLLRIGHT STONES

The Whispering Knights

A few battle-scarred stragglers defend the valley – twisting, turning, parrying, riposting an overwhelming enemy from behind the bent Victorian railings

There's a bench with a puzzling inscription and a softly spoken man – he came from London on a motorbike. I try to make conversation – that's not why he's here

I'll leave him to ask his question, hoping that the knights whisper back an answer shipping

shipping

shipping

shipping

shipping

62

Some young people, I hear, are into shipping.
Not all that stuff about tonnage and freight –
It's things like 'Lily ships James', or
'Merlin ships Arthur'. Relationships.

You see, some teenage bloggers are like trainspotters –
Completists, obsessive about facts and figures,
Whether it's Tolkien, Game of Thrones or Doctor Who.
But for other online fans, it's all about the human side …
Why does Remus look at Sirius that way?
It must be love. Love in all its forms –

Tender, at berth, and plain sailing
Love can be a destroyer too
What starts out wavy can soon turn rough
You go through hell and high water, to end up on the rocks.

Sometimes the world can seem like one big **BERMUDA**
LOVE TRIANGLE

You'd sooner walk the plank than walk down the aisle
Still you've got to take the plunge
You can't spend your whole life contemplating you're naval
Claiming you have a heart of oak
Or waiting for a dreamboat who turns out to be a hulk
You'll get cabin fever

As a child you dreamed of running away to sea
So run away with me
You've got to nail your colours to the mast …
Are you just cruising, frigate! – or is it maritime?

S*sorry*ying

It's what we're good at

First Great Western

Apologise for the recent flurry of apologies.

This is due to a delay on a previous apology *at Ealing Broadway.*

Rainy night
on the way
home

The
cars'
wet
eyes

flood

the
night
streets
one
after
another

3 Days in Lübeck

THE CHRISTMAS CAPITAL OF THE NORTH

We came here by train,
in the dark, but all the way
there were lights – on the trees,
in the windows – everywhere lit
up for Christmas.

Even before we got here,
you said 'Now you can see why
I love Christmas so much.'

DAY 1

At breakfast on the first day, it seems like every surface is crammed with decorations – scenes of children skating, or singing carols ... Not just a few baubles or bits of tinsel – if it can light up, or move, it'll do the lot.

Opposite the hotel, the bus station is festooned with fairy lights. You're triumphant – it's not like England. You say, 'I've seen that thing in Frideswide's Square – that's not a tree! Now *that's* a tree.'

In the Christmas market, the smell of apples and aniseed. The marzipan shop is being besieged by customers. I count them in at the rate of forty a minute. Only in Lübeck.

You say, 'My grandfather came here in the 1920s, when work on the land dried up. He was lucky – he found a job in a factory here.'

There's something of Manhattan about this place. The churches here are like cathedrals. In one, they're rehearsing Handel's 'Messiah'. In another, we're in time for candlelit Vespers. Music by Buxtehude – who was organist here – and Bach.

According to legend, the twenty-year-old Johann Sebastian walked five hundred miles – round trip, from Arnstadt – just to hear Buxtehude play, and to ask about a job, before leaving empty-handed. I think, 'Your grandfather was luckier than that.'

Saturday's icy, with flurries of snow. We take the train to Travemünde, where your uncle's family fled from the Soviets at the end of the war.

Today the town is full of shoppers, when suddenly a Father Christmas roars by on a motorbike, followed by a dozen others, all alike. I grab my camera and run after them – maybe I'll catch them at the lights! I haven't been so excited about seeing Father Christmas since I was five.

From Travemünde we take the clifftop path. You point out across the estuary, and say 'That used to be the East. When I was living here when I was twelve, there were soldiers on watchtowers all along that coast. If you went into the water, they'd shoot you.'

And to prove it, there's a monument – 'To those who found eternal peace in the Bucht' – and two middle-aged women standing there smoking, stony-faced. The candles are still burning – the flowers are fresh – the pain's still raw.

DAY 3

On our last full day, I walk to the station to check the trains. Bells are ringing out across the city.

At the station, there's the biggest single Christmas decoration I've ever seen, hanging from the ceiling – and nearby, a man with a clipboard and 'Refugees welcome' high-visibility jacket, surrounded by a bunch of kids looking lost. They're all so *young*.

That evening we walk into town one last time. An Italian restaurant – a party of students celebrating the end of term – a young waiter being berated by his boss.

I don't know what he's done, but he promptly knocks over a two-litre bottle of wine – tries to steady it – and sends another one flying. His boss practically propels him across the floor with rage.

The waiter's not German – you can tell from his accent. He looks Turkish – maybe Syrian.

His boss seems ready to spit blood again, when unexpectedly the students produce some crackers and pass them round. We get one, as do the waiter and his boss.

They pull it. The young man has won a thimble. He looks at it, then hands it to his boss, who bursts out laughing. It's hard to be mad with someone you've just pulled a cracker with. After that, the boy who could do no right can do no wrong. A little miracle of Christmas.

So now, if anyone says they don't believe in Christmas, I'll tell them 'I've seen it. And it's real.'

Frohe Weihnachten!

SHALL BE NAMELESS

Is it any coincidence that the poet William McGonagall
Had a name that rhymes with doggerel?
It's not a great rhyme,
But that's kind of the point.

In a world full of names, no one should be nameless.
Just hope your name doesn't rhyme with something rude –
A gift to playground bullies –
Or that you share a name with someone notorious,
And have strangers constantly asking
'Is that meant to be funny?'

When you choose your friends
Try and make sure they have unusual names
If you're planning to lose touch

Or you'll have trouble googling them in ten years' time.

Google Search   I'm Feeling lucky

If your surname's Conder,
Steer clear of women called Anna
If you have a name like Tom Phillips or Billy Collins,
                              and want to be famous
Try changing it to something that'll stick in people's minds.
Lucky for Andy Warhol and Benedict Cumberbatch –
They were born memorable.

And most importantly
Never entirely trust someone you've just met
Till they've asked your name, or told you theirs.

                                        Hi. My name's Ed.

The middle of this book
belongs to

....

Open
MIKE
night

Mike Richards was first up on stage. He bared his heart, confessing that he had ended all his relationships with women because he was physically more attracted to pianos.

Mike Sandwell was next up. He introduced the audience to his personal surgeon, who proceeded to perform heart surgery on Mike, live on stage.

Mike Allen, the owner of 'Mike's', the convenience store round the corner, was the final act on the bill. He announced that his shop was currently operative and would be 24/7 – until further notice.

BEING X & Z

X lives in a flat above Z in the arse-end of town.

They are outsiders, living an almost reclusive life away from the more popular K, F, C and hipsters like H and M.

They are seldom seen in the town centre, especially since Zara and TK Maxx closed down. In fact, X is barred from all the Italian restaurants and Z has a suspended sentence for stealing from M and S.

Of course, everything changed when the Scrabble championship came to town. Suddenly X and Z were more like VIPs. With 18 points combined, everybody wanted a piece of them.

The competition's sponsors B and H put them up in a luxury penthouse apartment, right in the centre, where C and A used to live.

On their first night there, X and Z got drunk with G and T, broke into VWs and went joyriding around the town, crashing into B and Q and ending the night lying in the beds of A and E.

They didn't care though. You see, X and Z are nonconformists, renegades, nihilists. In fact, they really couldn't give an FCUK.

LEBANESE FOOD

CENTRE

ACTON, NOVEMBER

Persimmons peaches oranges
defy the rain.

Inside ➜ chips and kebabs
tabouleh and Coca Cola™
the fiery unfamiliar script
small armies of tins
press against each other
pickles and preserves
Nescafé® and halva.
Steel skewers
sheathed in ground lamb
line up.
The brass trough
the red-hot charcoal.

He wraps the salad
tight in the thin bread
anoints with the lemon
tahini olive oil mix
cuts in two.

Swarthy silent men
draw their over-patterned knitwear
closer to their bodies.

Stubborn

It offends all fashion etiquette
But if socks with sandals fit the weather
Then that is what you'll get
Dress prohibitions are too much of a faff
Stubborn to the last
Will be my epitaph

The other night, I said too much
Last night I said too little
I'll say what I like, if only for a laugh
Monitoring my mouth is too much of a faff
Stubborn to the last
Will be my epitaph

We all suspect that Sky TV
Is an invitation to obesity
I say 'four channels if you will'
But leave it at that. I don't want a bigger bill
And learning the remote control is too much of a faff
Stubborn to the last
Will be my epitaph

to the

Never slow to condemn
A thing I've never tried
If you already know the answer
Why not make up your mind
Being open to discussion
is too much of a faff
Stubborn to the last
Will be my epitaph

People tell me that compared with beer
There's two thirds fewer calories in wine
That may be true, but the next pint's mine
Counting calories is too much faff
Stubborn to the last
Will be my epitaph

During a stay on these islands in 2012,
I experienced acute pareidolia – the
phenomenon of seeing faces/figures/
forms in random images, or patterns
of light and shadow …

Yes,
I saw the'
rocks
of St Agnes
&Gugh

I focused on a reclining Buddha
with the face of a gorilla
I giggled when I glanced
at a gleeful Godzilla

I met a former Teenage Mutant Ninja Turtle
who had just turned sixty-five
I discovered a Neanderthal
I couldn't believe was still alive

I caught sight of a twenty-foot-wide halibut
far too big for my pot
I witnessed Alfred Hitchcock
devising a maritime murder plot

I reflected on a winged serpent
silent in prayer
I worshipped at the temple
of the Hofmeister Bear

I disturbed a sleeping aardvark
or was it a meditating shrew?
Yes, I saw the rocks
of St Agnes and Gugh

I skirted around a Womble
who looked down on his luck
I came across an old man in shock
and asked him, 'What's up?'

I p-p-p-p-p-p-perceived a penguin
waiting patiently at a bar
I tried chatting to a parrot
but we didn't get very far

I bumped into a plump Snoopy
gorging on the gorse
I detected a face off the telly
but it wasn't Inspector Morse

I tiptoed past a lion
just for the thrill
I spied a spinosaurus
who looked ripe for the kill

I encountered a gladiatorial elephant
or was it a confused cockatoo?
Yes, I saw the rocks
of St Agnes and Gugh.

Sunset

IN A COUNTRYSIDE BEER GARDEN

Golden ales congregate
Under a pinkening sky
The sun setting on ashtrays
As conversation lights up
Gammon and chips* all round
Malt vinegar invades the nostrils
Sauce bottles are handed round
Red, brown, yellow and white
Peas are spilled on the table
Defective chips are abandoned
And it's dusk for dessert

Without a roof, laughter thrives
Even the dog turds can't soil the mood
And as we move into the night
Layers are added

*£6.50

LIFE IN THE 🚲 LANE

The sign says:

> **PEDESTRIANS**
> **LOOK**
> **RIGHT**

And I think: 'They so do.'

After a morning spent in suffocation

> **HOUSEBOUND** warding off talk
> of death and duty

> **I**
> **BREAK**
> **OUT** along Oxford Street on
> my bicycle – thinking we
> weren't born to be in the
> clutches of cars – screened
> from the wind, fair or ill

Sure, my bike
has gears, but
it's hard to **REMAIN**
NEUTRAL

Seeing eye to eye
with my fellow humans
Watching their indicators – **MAYBE**
A SMILE

Wondering if I know them, and discovering how quickly they look like **FRIENDS**

On the road, it seems the only certainties are cars and taxis But on the pavements

PEOPLE FLOW or **STAND AROUND** as if they're famous

It's like a festival Making **EYE CONTACT** without the risk of being chugged

These roads may take their toll But pedestrians can **COME AND GO**

And I can see from their eyes

WE'RE ALIVE

LIFE IN THE LANE

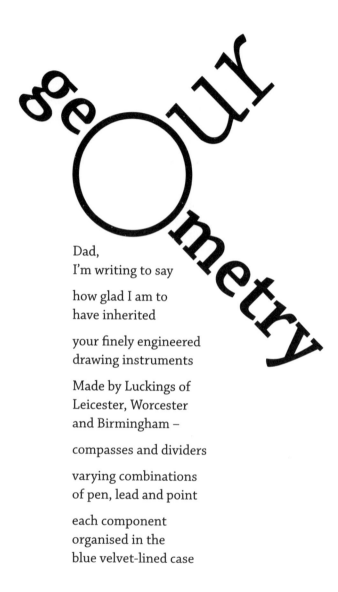

geOurometry

Dad,
I'm writing to say

how glad I am to
have inherited

your finely engineered
drawing instruments

Made by Luckings of
Leicester, Worcester
and Birmingham –

compasses and dividers

varying combinations
of pen, lead and point

each component
organised in the
blue velvet-lined case

I'm glad to have
your parallel rulers

the wood is dense
and dark

cool to the touch

the elegant hinges
are brass

a little tarnished
and ink-stained

I'm guessing you
believed in quality

in looking after things

in constructing the
answer with care
and precision

I never saw you draw.

Did one wild line
ever chase another?

If you ever start sketching

If you ever start sketching in a public place
You'll quickly draw a crowd
You may not be a master
But these people can be your subjects.
Immortalise them as they mill around
You'll notice something beautiful in all of them.

Action drawing can be quite a challenge.
I once tried to draw a man three times running
But I drew a blank. He was faster than me.
I couldn't catch his likeness.

Some people are born artists
My sister's been an artist since she first drew breath.
Most of us have to work at it
To see around that negative space
But don't worry if your still life goes pear-shaped
The imperfections are all part of the charm.

We all have our own individual style
You can picture yourself as something seismic
Rothko, Twombly or Gerhard Richter
But if you're honest, you'll end up being yourself.

Big bold statements or an eye for detail
Sombre and haunting or full of light
It's just you, and the moment
There's no better way to see, than like an artist
Sees the day.

Vegetarian paint
does not contain
pigment.

IN
MEMORY
OF
Ivor
Cutler

THE
FAKE
CUP

THE FIFTH ROUND DRAW FOR BOGUS FOOTBALL TEAMS

FOOL'EM	v	FARCENAL
NOT FOREST	v	NOT COUNTY
WEST SHAM	v	STRANGERS
NEVERTON	v	LESSER CITY
FIBERNIAN	v	OTHERWELL
BAYERN MIMIC	v	D'YOU INVENT US?
IPSWITCHED TOWN	v	CHARLATAN ATHLETIC
OXFORGED	v	BENFAKER

PROUDLY
SPONSORED BY

VODAPHONEY

91

DON'T RUSH TO

Even if you were Prince Llewelyn,
Would you leave your baby son and heir
To be looked after by a dog,
While you went hunting with your hawks
On the peaks of Moel Hebog?

And, if Gelert was a hunting dog,
Why was he not with you?

And where was Mrs Llewelyn?

And if, on your return,
The baby's cot was empty, bloody,
And Gelert, blood-grimed,
Leapt at you in anxious welcome,

JUDGEMENT

Would you assume you knew so clearly
Both the crime, and the culprit
That you speared your trusted dog
Through his faithful heart?

Only to find, once your eyes
Became accustomed to the dark,
A terrified but unharmed child
And the torn and lifeless body
Of a wolf.

The Dutiful Game

This is just to say thanks, son,

For being so crap at football

For not making me stand

In the cold and the rain

Cheering on your team

Like all those other dads.

Cricket was more your thing.
Standing in a field, chatting to your mates
And the chance afterwards of a can of coke ...

That's roughly how far my own interest in sport extends –
Relaxing in the sunshine with a glass of something cold,
Watching other people throwing themselves around.

They think we're being sporting as we clap the other side
But in truth we don't really care about the result
So long as no one dies, and we've got a drink ...
Who's winning? I'm not even sure who's playing.

I could listen to the Test Match Special team for ever
Adelaide sunshine warming our longer winter nights
It's one of the few things, apart from sleeping,
That's even better with your eyes shut.

Cricket – you even helped bring down Apartheid.
That's the kind of result worth caring about.
Still, it's good to see you other dads cheering on your boys
I may even ask you who's winning
As I walk on by.

A mobile phone sales team
From electronics firm Samsung
Sailed to the Isles of Scilly
And an island called Samson

Arriving on the shore
The salesmen were all at sea
For not a soul was waiting
To buy the Galaxy S3

In inappropriate beachwear
The suits of DKNY
They waited for customers
But only hours passed them by

Being on commission
They were desperate to sell
So they left the beach behind
In search of clientele

4

SALESMEN FROM SAMSUNG

SAILED TO AN ISLAND CALLED SAMSON

Two hills dominate the island
And the first one they climbed
They met Heather and Iris
But, alas, not the human kind

Ascending the second hill
Heavy fog from all around
Swallowed up the salesmen
And never were they found

But for one day, every May
When night draws near
On top of that second hill
Four silhouettes appear

The four salesmen of Samsung
Are now contract free
They stand with the guillemots
And stare out to sea.

12 tablespoons of absinthe

1 tab of acid

1 psychotic swimming attendant

Half a leisure centre
(the swimming pool half)

40kg of hot chilli powder

700 soluble aspirins

50 human beings

120 banana skins

12 tigers (starved for 48 hours)

1 star anise

A recipe for disaster

walcot

Dozing cows, eyes lashed like daisies
And browner than caramel
Waiting for the world to turn
And bring another tongue-twist of grass
Beneath their mouths

Skellig

As the second gin and tonic from Heathrow
Smoothes the plane's path to the New World
Look down to see the Old one slip quietly away
In a shrinking line of land, ending in two full-stops
Before the unpunctuated Atlantic:
Europe's last lonely rocks

The next time I saw the Skelligs was in a holy roller,
                                  post-storm swell
That had been born near Boston,
No G&Ts to smooth the small boat's course.
Where Brân the Blessed might have flung
A Snowdon range into the ocean,
Rising above the waves are only craggy summit rocks

Great Skellig's seven hundred feet of sandstone grit
Is scaled by steps that creep towards the narrow ledge
Where beehive huts perched above the drop
Cling defiant like limpets to the rocks

Otherwise, in all the time that makes up
               seven centuries, in all that time
The monks left only cramped and rudimentary
                     burial grounds
Where wind and rain have scoured the headstones clean
Of any clue to why they so loved this savage place
That stinks of gannets
And where only sea pink, campion and scurvy grass
                    grow on the rocks

Tortured by the sight of mainland shores
Whipped into submission by lashing rain and wind,
Was it to punish or to purify themselves,
Or just to know the loneliness of God,
That they chose to live and die upon these rocks?

THE HALLOUMI HOOLIGAN

I don't care for Camembert
I'm not a fan of Parmesan
Caerphilly? Don't be silly

HALLOUMI HALLOUMI HALLOUMI

Grill it, griddle it
Fritter it, pitta it
A slug of oil, chilli and lemon
I must have fried and gone to heaven

HALLOUMI HALLOUMI HALLOUMI

It's better than Feta
Squeaks louder than Gouda
I'd probably snort it
If it came in a powder

HALLOUMI HALLOUMI HALLOUMI

Monterey Jack? I ain't 'avin that
Mozzarella? Not this fella
Davidstow? I wouldn't stoop so low
Cathedral City? More's the pity
Port Salut? I ask you
And Danish Blue can piss off too

HALLOUMI HALLOUMI HALLOUMI

Barbecued or in a stew
Is there anything it cannot do?
Perhaps with biscuits it might not agree
But I'd still take it over Stilton and Brie

HALLOUMI HALLOUMI HALLOUMI

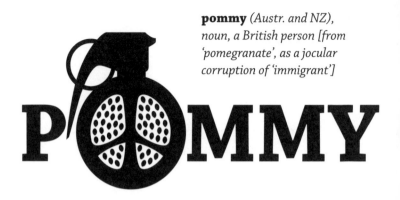

pommy (Austr. and NZ), noun, a British person [from 'pomegranate', as a jocular corruption of 'immigrant']

P🅾MMY

He had it all planned, this Londoner
How he'd explode onto the Sydney scene
With his beats, with his freestyle
Like a bolt from the blue.
Australia was booming, by all reports …
Highly charged and fully primed
He'd burst into fame
His words would be dynamite
A muse with a short fuse –
He'd blow them all away.
With spraypaint he'd bomb the bridges, hard as granite
His killer drawings would be sharp one-liners
His portrait would be blown up on every billboard.
He might even find an Aussie girl – she'd be a cracker …
It was going to be a blast.

grenade, *noun, a small bomb thrown by hand [from Fr. grenade, Sp. granada, pomegranate]*

GRENADE

But in reality he found Sydney
Ticking over quite well without him.
For the most part,
People left him to his own suspect devices
Like a time bomb that has passed its use-by date
His art was a damp squib
His rap, all bombast
And when he tried to propel himself into the limelight
His plans backfired. It was a minefield.
He found the doors barred by the Grenadine guards
The stalwarts of the scene exploded his dreams,
They blew him off
And gave him a dishonourable discharge.
He needed revenge –
It's better to burn out than to fade away

And then one ordinary Monday morning
Without so much as a telephoned warning
He just
         went
                off.

All is well and go‑d
in Lucca

Zita was born in Tuscany, spent her life in domestic service in Lucca, and subsequently became the patron saint of housemaids. She is portrayed in a medieval wall painting in the church of All Saints, Shorthampton, West Oxfordshire.

The marbled streets still cool, an early,
Lemon-yellow Tuscan sun
That matches the plane trees' changing shade
Shines through Zita's window in the wealthy weaver's house –
Almost a halo around her bed –
And rouses the maid to her daily job of baking bread

Later, in the cellar kitchen,
Kneading flour and water in the trough
Zita is distracted from the dough
And goes to attend a beggar knocking at the door.
She is known by all – despised by some –
For her attention to the poor

In spite, a servant tells the Lady of the house
That Zita, neglectfully, has given up her task.
While others must work to meet the household's needs
She spends her time in self-indulgent deeds

The mistress storms down the stairs.
But, when she sees the kitchen,
Holds her hands in wonder to her head.
Amid an urgent whispering of wings,
Angels are busy baking Zita's bread.

Alfred,
what is there for you here?
I had a bad feeling
as we came down the steep
Barnoon Hill to The New Place
steel, glass and concrete.
Your tiny frame drowns beside it.
It was wrong to wake you from
dreams of Newfoundland
and the Madron workhouse.
What is there for a God-fearing man?
The sugar still tastes of slavery.
There's no tea-treat bun
or Mrs Wallis's heavy cake,
no dish of Christian tea.
What is there for a cabin-boy,
a fisherman, a rag-and-bone man
who painted on cardboard
to keep the sadness away.

**With Alfred
Wallis at
Tate St Ives**

John Lanyon
2018
words on paper

NIL BY MOUTH

Allow me a language or two
but spare me the yearning of deep tongues

If I had as many lives as I have bags for life I'd be well on my way to immortality or do I mean reincarnation

ANOTHER ANOTHER ANOTHER

bag life

coming back as a butterfly, or maybe as a Beatle

Or even a member of One Direction
A former boy band, now with added trumpets
To announce their resurrection.

Sure, it bothers me sometimes
That lots of these bags
Come from shops that no longer exist
Ottakar's ... Woolworths ... BHS ...
I mean you wouldn't buy elocution lessons
From a Trappist monk
So why stake your hopes of immortality
On something that's defunct?

And yet the sight of all these bags
Hanging from the pantry door
Makes me think that after all
There may be something more
So when your life seems to be draining away
And you're struggling to cope
Remember – while you've got a bag for life
You've still got hope.

Leaves wave sarcastically

Empty cars, lining the street

Temporary metallic gravestones

Registration plates reveal their age

A windscreen cinema   An empty space amongst the metal

Previewing winter   And a large sign that pulls no punches

The air is bitterly cold   **DO NOT PARK IN FRONT OF GATE**

The sky is seal grey   Painted in Dulux 'Don't fuck with us' Red

Mid-summer observations from...

Pigeons shiver
On the scaffolding
Eyeing up Dorito crumbs
Chilli flavoured – fittingly

A workman feeds a trailer   The workman calls up his wife
And shouts to a passer-by: 'Let's put the heating on tonight
'It feels more like December'   And have stew and dumplings'
She smiles politely and walks on.   **The wind howls in triumph.**

… a parked car in Leamington Spa

1

First response
a smile.

First answer,
yes.

First reaction,
I love it. Because.

st

RESPONSE
QUICK REACTION CUE CARD

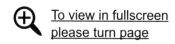

ROOMINATING

Standing in my sitting room, I thought to myself, I'd never actually dined in my dining room. Breakfast and lunch, yes, but never dinner. It also occurred to me, I'd never studied in my study – just emailed and watched videos of dogs falling over on YouTube.

I had no pencils or paper in my drawing room and I'd never bathed in my bathroom – it only had a shower. I hadn't even got a bed in my bedroom – I sleep on a chaise-longue.

I further concluded I'd never lobbied for anything in my lobby, I had no cloaks in my cloakroom, no lard lurking in my larder and no jam in my conservatory.

I decided I wasn't using my house appropriately so I sold up and went to live in a brothel – where I now spend my days consuming bowls of thin watery soup.

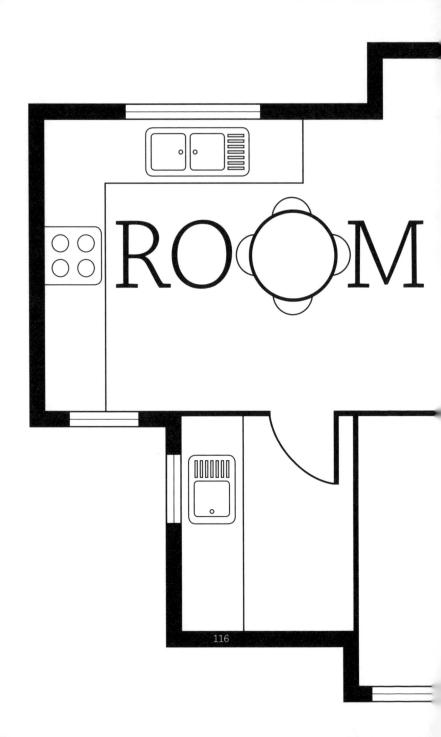

INATING

Standing in my sitting room, I thought to myself, I'd never actually dined in my dining room. Breakfast and lunch, yes, but never dinner. It also occurred to me, I'd never studied in my study – just emailed and watched videos of dogs falling over on YouTube.

I had no pencils or paper in my drawing room and I'd never bathed in my bathroom – it only had a shower. I hadn't even got a bed in my bedroom – I sleep on a chaise-longue.

I further concluded I'd never lobbied for anything in my lobby, I had no cloaks in my cloakroom, no lard lurking in my larder and no jam in my conservatory.

I decided I wasn't using my house appropriately so I sold up and went to live in a brothel – where I now spend my days consuming bowls of thin watery soup.

festival construction

We weren't raised by wolves, lads –
At least not me –
But today my middle name is Romulus
And you can be Remus
As we take these soft green fields
And build a city here between us.

It's not meant to last a thousand years
In fact, just one weekend
Then we'll take it down, and in a year
We'll start it all again.

And this year's serfs will be next year's kings
Reputations made and shattered
But as actors come and actors go
It's the stage alone that matters.

LIFE AND **DEATH** ON A SMALL TOWN FILM SET

Charlbury's a funny place …
Sometimes, walking around town,
I feel as if I'm on the set of a movie
Only no one's given me the script. So what's the film?

You see, we're Eight Mile
North by Northwest, of
Woodstock
In the former parliamentary constituency of
The Decameron.
This is England,
But sometimes it feels like all the Ordinary People
Have been Spirited Away
As if everyone you meet is Almost Famous.

If you go to The Rose – that's our local –
Chances are you'll bump into The Artist,
Mick Rooney RA,
Talking about The Last Picture Show of his.
If you go to the station, you'll find that
The Constant Gardener
Is none other than former royal consort
Roddy Llewellyn, of all people …
And while you're down there
Look out for Jack Straw and Douglas Hurd
Treating each other like Strangers on a Train.

I N T E R M I S S I O N

And as for our GPs ...
There's the one who's always telling me to slow down –
The one who says I should love my neighbour –
And the one who'll never write me a sick note.
I call them Dr Dolittle, Dr Strangelove, and Dr No.

And if this is a film, is it some kind of classy society
drama – a rural idyll – or something a whole lot darker?
How come so many people here have links with Oxford,
The fictional murder capital of the world?
Why does the director of 'Midsomer Murders' have a
house here? And why have the other pub quiz teams
taken to calling me The Man Who Knew Too Much?

And now just recently, walking around town,
I've started feeling that I'm on a film set
Where everyone has the script except me ...
That in this film
I'm destined to make only the very briefest appearance
In the opening shot of the first scene
As the latest member of ...
The Dead Poets Society.

F   I   N

AT THE ROLLRIGHT STONES

The King Stone

It is
evening,
the game of
summer nearly done,
all your pieces taken,
you against the black queen.
She didn't play fair, wearing
a dress like that – she's still
playing with you. I have
been a king. I have
been bewitched.
I have been a
standing stone.
I reach out to you,
remember your warmth,
sense your weight, invite the
lines in your face to soften.

Young mums
feed their babies
in the art gallery

Before the protest
policemen eat Walkers crisps
in their big white van

IN THE CITY

Unshaven, homeless
big ticks
on his Nikes

My neighbour's post falls
onto my doormat –
So that's her name

The railway pigeons
refuse to follow
the new timetable

They missed the play
a suicide on the line
Waiting for Godot

A businesswoman
her stockinged feet on the train seat
planning the future

IN THE CITY

The drunken   architect
searches
for his house

Epitaph

Later
People will remember just
two things about our lives
If we're lucky.

One will be not quite right
The other will be something
to make people laugh.

A GAME OF CARDS
with Fred Damek

'Fred Damek, of Chicago, compiled a
complete pack of cards by picking them
up from time to time in the street.'
(From 'The Omnibus Believe It or Not'
by Robert L. Ripley, 1934)

It would have been the strangest game
Texas hold 'em, not a chance
Every card from a different pack
And with different patterns on the back.

Still I craved a mad deck like Damek's ...
My first card was the knave of clubs
And in the twenty years since then
I've found a nine and a pair of tens.

Four cards that random people dropped
Spades, diamonds, clubs ... and then it stopped
Quite heartlessly, and here's the choker –
Not even enough for a hand of poker.

I kept searching: but two, three, four and five
Failed miserably to arrive.
Nothing was at sixes and sevens.
As for eight, seems I'll have to wait.
A republic – no kings or queens –
And certainly no aces up my sleeve.

Then it struck me. It's not a game, it's destiny
But why had fate dealt me this hand?
My jack, Google says, is Lancelot
But the other three mean not a jot.

And when all four are placed together?
I was desperate for an answer …
But no. 'Your search returned no results.'
I felt discarded – desolate.

Was Lancelot ever told such a thing
In his search for the Holy Grail?
Once a quest could last a lifetime …
Maybe it was easier then

To go through life believing in some meaning?
All I can do is keep on hoping
That somehow, somewhere, something will turn up
To make sense of my busted flush.

Lyssos

The ancient Greek and Roman city of Lyssos, set in a remote part of southern Crete, was once a port large enough to mint its own coins. Today only vestiges remain.

LYSSOS
PAST

The fields are bright with yellow asphodel
and singing birds
Set among shimmering oleander groves
and healing springs
Marble fountains overflow
The city thrives
The headlands point to Africa, but ships
come from every quarter
Wharves stacked with wool and oil and wine
Black olives fall thick
An amber necklace bartered for a sailor's kiss
Temples where many come with offerings
Even the dead have a view of the sea
The theatre sounds with lyre and flute
Butterflies as blue as iris

LIZARDS ALONE EXPLORE THE CRACKS

LYSSOS
PRESENT

Among the stinkhorn lily

Bleats an orphaned kid

Terraces lie bare

Deep we dig for any scent of moisture

Empty cisterns amplify the hiss of snakes

The city dies

No sign of sail, where the sky dissolves

into the water

The harbour silts as the sea declines

Our oil jars empty

A shipwrecked mariner, black and bloated; the only pearls his eyes

A gold amulet falls and is lost to the ground

Robbed mausoleums

Empty thunder in the hills; sky red dust; another month of drought

The few drops of rain form spots of blood

Asklepios sleeps. The gods are gone

BETWEEN THE PRESENT AND THE PAST

NEARLY IN
conclusion

'love'

at the end of a letter.
A verb missing a noun?
A noun floating in space?
An ancient suitcase
where we keep
all the things
we meant to say.

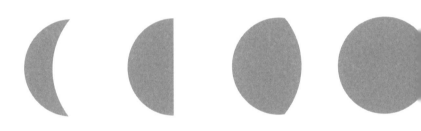

At a time when animals would have us for prey
The full moon was invitation to the feast
Perhaps that is why we feared it
And positioned gods to absorb its rays

To the Chinese, the moon is a hare
To Africans a woman; to us a man
And cheese; sometimes Cheddar
But, low on the horizon, definitely Double Gloucester

Was it really the steadying attraction of this moon
That slowed our planet's spinning
And allowed life to develop – without a headache

It was the moon

All of this is *so* unlikely N

And it was also the unlikely development of water.
The creator Goldilocks found
At an improbably exact distance
The third stone from the sun
Where there was neither vapour nor ice

And we should not forget
The random passage of a wandering star
That nudged the gassy planets into wider orbit
Saving us from their bloated digestion

All of this is so unlikely
Can we really   be   here   at   all   ?

what's whose?

ADRIAN LANCINI

A writer's notebook

No fires: No camping

A piece of cake

A toucan in Sheffield

Pub quiz

Dear old Oxford

Open Mike Night

Being X & Z

Yes, I saw the rocks
of St Agnes and Gugh

Sunset in a countryside
beer garden

The FAKE Cup

Four salesmen from Samsung
sailed to an island called Samson

A recipe for disaster

The Halloumi hooligan

Mid-summer observations from
a parked car in Leamington Spa

Roominating

EDWARD FENTON

The soul's last words
to the heart

Reuse, reduce and recycle

We are all continuing
the journeys of others

Who knows where the car goes

Shipping

Three days in Lübeck

Who shall be nameless

Life in the bike lane

If you ever start sketching

The dutiful game

Pommy grenade

Another bag, another life

First response quick reaction
cue card

Festival construction crew

Life and death on a
small town film set

Epitaph

A game of cards with Fred Damek

JOHN LANYON

The standardisation of raindrops

Salon

To be

Festival

At the Rollright Stones:
The King's Men

Finding myself alone
in the museum

Ghostwriting the ghostwriter

On the horizon

Crossing

On the passing of the F1350APW

The Whispering Knights

Saying sorry –
it's what we're good at

Rainy night on the way home

Lebanese Food Centre

Our geometry

In memory of Ivor Cutler

With Alfred Wallis
at Tate St Ives

The King Stone

In the city

Nearly in conclusion

ROB STEPNEY

The providence of birds

A message for our times

Love hearts

Flowers of Sutjeska

Is a path the wisdom
of many feet?

Carrara

An unseen hand

Withdrawal

Stubborn to the last

Don't rush to judgement

Walcot

Skellig

All is well and good in Lucca

Nil by mouth

Lyssos

Moon

Messages of thanks...

Jon Carpenter

Many thanks for publishing our first book 'A Funny Way with Words'.

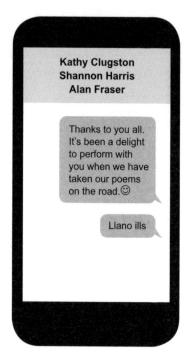

Kathy Clugston
Shannon Harris
Alan Fraser

Thanks to you all. It's been a delight to perform with you when we have taken our poems on the road.☺

Llano ills

**The Editors of
Obsessed with Pipework
The Sandspout
The Stare's Nest
The Poetry Shed**

Thank you for
including some
of these poems in
your publications.
📖💻

Countless Others

We couldn't have
done it without you.
👍👍👍👍👍
👍👍👍👍👍
👍👍👍👍👍
👍👍👍👍👍
👍👍👍👍👍
👍👍👍👍👍
👍👍👍👍👍
👍👍👍👍👍
👍👍👍👍👍
👍👍👍👍